DEVIL, Dear

DEVIL, *Dear*

MARY ANN MCFADDEN

ALICE JAMES BOOKS

FARMINGTON, MAINE

10 9 8 7 6 5 4 3 2 1

Alice James Books are published by Alice James Poetry Cooperative, Inc., an affiliate of the University of Maine at Farmington.

Alice James Books
114 Prescott Street
Farmington, ME 04938
www.alicejamesbooks.org

Library of Congress Cataloging-in-Publication Data

McFadden, Mary Ann.
  [Poems. Selections]
  Devil, Dear / Mary Ann McFadden.
      pages cm
  ISBN 978-1-938584-08-4 (paperback)
  I. Title.
  PS3613.C4374A6 2014
  811'.6--dc23
                            2014010127

Alice James Books gratefully acknowledges support from individual donors, private foundations, the University of Maine at Farmington, and the National Endowment for the Arts.

ART WORKS.
arts.gov

Cover Art: "Angel's Tear" by Sarah McCabe

Table of Contents

Acknowledgments

Grateful acknowledgment is made to the editors of the following journals and anthologies, in which some of these poems first appeared (sometimes in earlier versions) for their generous support of this work.

Green Mountains Review: "How Lightning Strikes," "Devil, Dear,"
    "That Year the Whales," "Animal Warmth," "At Risk," "Did You Ever"
Psychology Tomorrow Magazine: *At the Intersection of Art and Psychology*: "Night Windows," "In Phoebus' Car"
Southern Poetry Review: "Disco Saturday Night"
The Marlboro Review: "To the Lizard God"
BLOOM: "Like Candles," "Roosters," part 2 of "Baja Eclogue"
The American Voice: "Marriage"
Willow Springs: "Goodbye"
Snowy Egret: "Having Murdered 23 Slugs"
Moving Out: "Fire in the Canyon"

"After the Crash the Old Fool Does Laundry" was anthologized in *The Arc of Love: An Anthology of Lesbian Love Poems,* edited by Claire Coss (Scribner, 1996).

"Marriage" was anthologized in *My Lover Is a Woman,* edited by Leslea Newman (Ballantine Books, 1996).

"Crickets" was set to music by the composer Gerald Busby and was performed at the Carnegie Center, New York City, 2005.

My heartfelt thanks to The MacDowell Foundation for the precious gift of support and for the time during which several of these poems were written.

I am especially grateful to the following friends and family, some of whom read my manuscript in one of its many forms, or who helped with love and support, or who said the right thing when I most needed to hear it: Sarah McCabe, Geoff McCabe, Martha Kazlo, Leslie Hall Pinder, Judy Klein, Dorothy Leland, Carolyn McCabe, Tom Wilson, Anne Lewis, Joy Wesson, Beatriz Garcia Sainz, Gwen Deely, Rae Wilken, Merilie Robertson, Norma Jane, Anya Hunter, Carolyn Kizer, Laura Juliet Wood, Lynn Wetzel.

Huge thanks to Tamiko Beyer for her careful eye, and to Carey Salerno, Alyssa Neptune, and all the editors at Alice James Books.

*For my children, Geoffrey David McCabe
and Sarah Elizabeth McCabe*

To the Lizard God

God of damnation, lizard god eaten alive each day by the cat
and your guts ground into the carpet, or flung, O god
of abandonment, into a corner, god of stench, god of retribution,

warm and soft in my paper napkin, tossed in the wastebasket,
carried out with crumbs and paint flakes, fruit skins
and onion husks, nail parings and hair fished from drains,

with crushed bugs and blooded, swatted, stinging things,
O god that gives and takes away, forget me in your pain,
turn your face from me in your suffering,
close your eyes upon me in the furnace of midday

as you begin to rot, or in the tepid rain.
When ants deliver your flesh to their queen, when your acids
leak into dirt, when your frail bones fall into calcium

and enter the clear blood of plants, when you are sipped
at last to the top of the tree, think of me, O infant,
when the brown moth alights on you and you give thanks,
O god of the one everlasting touch, O breath, remember me.

I long for the imperishable quiet at the heart of form.

—Theodore Roethke

Animal Warmth

Is it my imagination, or do the deer's coats darken in winter?

Sweetheart, what I said on the phone about sharing a bed together,
that fear of insomnia that haunts me like a gravy stain,
I was wrong to mention it. Forgive me. Truly, I've learned
that sleeping with you is what I wanted all along.

My years of restless nights were caused by the dearth of you beside me,
as if I knew you were there, behind a screen, and couldn't reach you.

What matters most as we step delicately into our thicket,
our dark coats exactly the shade of dampened bark, is the certainty
that we are truer together than we are alone.

So if I wake you as I thrash to widen my small dent in the snow,
or if you wake me throwing your arm over my chest,
I trust I can fall asleep again, can rest because of your breathing,
your particular snore-note,

and that the beasts I fear, the wolf, the hunter—though they will find us
one night, and first one of us, then the other, will be taken—

I don't have to think about it now, not tonight, not this year
as we climb into our covers and fall deep into the snowy woods,
into animal warmth, sleepers and lovers.

Someplace to Go

In a wave, in a jumble of brass rings,
like a sputtering diffusion of gas, the things of this world pass by me.

The things of this world fill me up
like a sunbeam falling down the side of an empty cup
clear to the cool, flat bottom.

                    Behold this mechanical toothache,
this tub of parts that flutter momentarily in the air over the bumps
until wrench and lug bolts hit the floor with a gratified crunch—

we are old, we are young, with a flip of the thumb: the impermanently
earthbound, duct-taped cloud of our very own vehicular apparatus!

Oh the spun, hinged winds we shape with our own hands. Ah, we lunge,
fan fanatically forward toward what positively sobs to be done.

Highly decorated, serenely plushed, of temperamental chrome
and with swaths of batteries burning.

                    Now we see through the dark.
We move along just as we intended, we've turned the corner just

as we predicted, we lift off, buoyed by the somewhat
appalling thunder of our engines

Did You Ever

walk past the house of someone you wanted to know,
admire the yard, glimpse figures waltzing inside the windows?

If you've been a long time at sea, or lost anywhere at all,
you understand the hope I feel when I open a book I've begun.
I'm looking for a port, a friendship, a meal, an erotic coupling.

And it can't be rushed, like space travel, light years, until the poems
are part of my breathing: like galaxies, they contract and expand.

One, hidden behind the bright face of the one before it,
goes unnoticed, and then, shy mouse, catches my attention.

Now and again I see mistakes the poet made, not mistakes but blurts,
egoistic slips or failures of nerve. Little cracks in the verse
through which I enter, through which the poem gives birth.

There was a poet, now dead, who, in life I loved from afar, not love,
it was infatuation, what else could it have been from such a distance?
Though we did take a few meals together, and kissed once or twice.

I dreamed he humbly came to me—we'd begun together at last.
But I awoke before the love scene, awoke in my mosquito net
bestirred by the overhead fan, pulled myself up to feed the cats
and so the day began. But we met. Beloved man, we met again.

I didn't know what I wanted. It's so much easier, isn't it,
to please someone else than to say wait, not yet, I'm not certain.

He was such a rake. What would I have meant to him?

I wanted to believe I would be the one he grew to comprehend
once he had failed with all the others, as I had failed with others,
though not that many times.

                    I bring my conflicting emotions
to the books I read, and sometimes the words take fire. As, yesterday,
I was seethingly envious as a poem I wished to have written

turned and turned and finally brought me, shriven, into its arms.

At Risk

So here we are, the fortunate who live on past the rest
into old age, and why are we still such fools?
All those years of love and sex, or just love, or just sex,
or great sex, or not-so-great sex—what does it add up to?

My kids are gliding in the gusts of their lives,
swift and daredevil! When I taught them to ride a bike,
I ran holding them steady with my hand on the seat.
When I felt their balance, I quietly let go.
They'd been riding a while before they knew it.

I don't want to put too much weight on my love for you,
yet I'm curious to see where this might lead,
amazed as the wave of my elder self lifts me up.
I'm wearing my nephew's surfer sweatshirt
here at my desk, my funny, old body in precarious balance,
as the swell breaks and I hang on for dear life.

Or say it's a new kind of grace
not to know what you can do and what you can't.

I saw a film last night about elephants. Motion, but also stills
in black and white that captured the flow, that caught the delicate

poise of their indecision, legs picked up and set down like courtesans,
aware of their bodies in space and aware of time.

The day before Christmas, my children's father collapsed.
First our son, then our daughter, flew up to keep him company
and help make decisions. But they're not staying in touch.

It's true their father and I have been divorced for 30 years,
but I loved him once, and I wish him well. I spent Christmas
with friends, but still I wanted to talk with them.

Some of the older elephants had broken or missing tusks.
The filmmaker showed the herd in motion
like a form of water both fluid and dense,
swinging their weight gracefully, power in perfect balance.

They rocked and sailed all at once.
I am the boat and I am the ocean.

One old matriarch gave birth to her eighth child.
All the other females gathered around weeping a liquid
from a gland in their cheeks. They rumbled and called

as within their protective circle of tree trunks, the newborn child
ripped his membrane, struggled to rise, and rose

while emotional mountains bumped each other, sisters and aunts
danced with the new baby, stroked and adored him,
welcomed him with trumpets.

Talking idly of how we wished to die, I said
I wanted to be devoured by lions alone in the mountains
of North America. It seemed a noble death, my friends agreed,

but the next day I was bitten by a dog as we raced for an orange
floating in the pool. The accidental bite sent a shock
from my hand all the way to my elbow, and changed my mind.

After drinking and bathing and plunging around hilariously
in the river, the family turned back toward the dry
valley where there were trees and shrubs to eat.

They met a lone female and her ill and starving child.
All of them stopped, they knew one other, and talked for a while.

The lone elephant was tempted to turn and join them,
but she and her child needed water, so they went on.
A few days later, the child of the lone elephant died.

But the film was over, and nobody saw where the mother went.
To be alone is to be at risk. Lions and tigers.

To begin again now, after this year of being friends,
to approach from different ends of the earth, sleep in the same
bed sometimes after a life wandering in and out of the crowd—

I'm not inexperienced, but I'm new at being wise,
new at patience, new at this forbearance you require.

I don't know how to do this, you said at the very beginning,
and who knows what smart-sounding thing I replied.

The Children of
John Farlo's Wife

The older one was five, and she knew what to do.
The younger child cried at first, but they made a plan.

Each day they would scratch a hole in which to hide their excrement,
and the next day another hole beside it. It was a measure,
and it would tell them how long they had been alone.

Because there was only a little bag of corn, they were careful
not to eat too much, and so the pit was fairly clean.

Their mother had cut agave leaves for them to chew
and suck, and at night the moisture formed droplets on the leaves
which they could lick. To not have food was not unusual,

and they didn't need much. They were shaded and cool
as they touched one another and watched the daylight creep down the walls,
filling the pit west to east. The children grew so still

they could hear a beetle running over the dirt, and the wingbeats
of mounting birds. They felt the actual weight of the moon
and listened to the knuckles of growing roots. The stars traced across

their upturned faces and marked them for life.
The hooves of their parents' horses vibrated a long way off,
but the children didn't move and didn't cry out.

When the ladder came down and they were hoisted
and rubbed with rough hands, and wrapped and put by a fire,
they began to wake in a new way, like Mars in his orbit
spinning back, wise after his journey to the end of space.

They were brand new, they were ancient, they were true.
They knew they were true.

Late in the Day

I'm reading it again, the best book, the very best book I ever read.

Then, I was young.
I wished for magic, longed for magic, nobility, and scope.
Now I mourn the loss of magic.
Now I see it everywhere, more than ever now, I think.

Over the hills to the east, pale oceans float. Shifting lines of ibis
by the hundreds cross over us in vees, in waves, in chords.

A neighbor's red wall. A sudden patch of light.
A shadow jumps into it. Lifts its arms.
Pulls a shadow shirt out of the sky.
Falls down out of sight.

On window glass,   on balconies,   reflected pinks.
A solitary ibis flies as fast as he can, maybe he's not too late.

The sun is down.   Everything stops.   And starts again
as I flip on my electric lights, sadder now, a bit more quiet.

My book is here.   I pick it up.   But I'm not sure,
not quite sure I want to read it.

Hung Not Plumb

Despite my ignorance of love, or even friendship,
my feral upbringing half-lost in the hills and mountains,
dunced by the hard-eyed towns, judgments, restrictions of church
and school, though there was always kindness for the asking,
always a cup of cool water,
                      though you won't forgive me in this life,
I'm thankful to you who first heard my voice, who risked with me.
I was chained and gagged, I was a block of wood.

I bless you for throwing me away — though the river I drowned in
was brackish and ribboned with bitter juices and every word I wrote
was self-preservation, then discovery, then discipline, puffery,
despair, longing, then the long thirst and self-flagellation—
nothing was lost, nothing was quite lost.

Out of the need to be large, out of the pretense of wisdom,
the exhaust of imagination, floats this hulk
battered and spare and generous.
                      Not the rare and precious wing,
but desperate, dulled, enduring, cast from tin and lead, hung not plumb,
still hacking at the dirt with a sword, planting with a bandaged thumb.

Faith in Nights

In this hearing of quiet drums and quiet piano,
hushed marimba, tin pan,
furnace whistling off and on in a flush of air,
air withdrawn,

jazz dance and stumbling down the stairs,
bicycles and wood fires, blessed naps and imaginary bears,

she sits down at her desk
and begins to play the keys of another music.

The beat of her heart is strong and sure.
Her socks wave like wind flags over an old airport.

She arrives at the pure aboriginal.
She tracks the spoor,
the disturbed twig, the bruised leaf on the stone.

Once again she comes to the end of what went before.

She pulls off her elastic, her tight watch,
the body breathes and beats like a shy animal behind a bush

as she passes it, the quavers and semi-quavers of her light
along the sandy road,
moisture flowing around her: she walks on water.

The conifers hover above her in a neutral amazement,
a noncombatant participatory story they make
and hear simultaneously

as the breeze of her passing brushes them,
the breath of her body greets their transpiration.

Beyond them the morning frost
is not settling, nor poised above the meadow,
nor even barely coalescing.

To Break It to Find It Again

Not always, but always. Including death-arousing noise:
jerk and robot—both the *no* and the *yes*.
Oddly new, newly old: to find the flirt in us.

If poodle can prance, can prong, if squirrel,
if ocean's brilliant foam is thin enough to breathe.

Wise animal music pumped out in pups, kits, chicks, drips.
If turtle hatchlings blunder, magnets for the salt sea.

If we are lost, far from the breast. Too far up. Away far down.
And then trees, giants, and also the tiny wild blooms.

She opens her eyes. In her water we see us: vulvaed creatures
by the ocean that are the ocean. They taste of her. Tits and pips,
mountainous crusts and secretions. Birthing eyes of the divine.

If we wash away, if we melt, if we are clumsy and hilarious.
Splayed feet, we quack. If we are a parade of elephants

linked trunk to tail. If we are continents balanced on a ball.
If we are clapping, sucking in our next first breath.

That Year the Whales

That year the whales rose out of the green paint,
I forgot to hate the things I used to hate.

I left the wallpaper hanging in strips and let the cats
go in and out while books piled up in drifts.
That year, I let myself stay up late and drink,
though the clock that rang at six was loudly cursed.

That was the year the children's rooms began to reek
of moldering oranges and chocolate.

And I had yet to write a thousand stupid lines about love,
that impossible give and take, though I and a friend
took time enough to understand the words we couldn't say.

All that spring the shadows made a changing shape
on the neighbor's clapboard walls: like rows of ocean waves

where blisters from the summer sun began to swell
with a cetacean grace, and let their bellies roll.
I watched out my window while the slow months' weight,
that year the whales rose out of the green paint,

pressed like coal in my throat, until the whole year lit up,
and dove, and shrank itself to a minute.

Letter, April 12

Will it really be September before I see you again?
We will have moved north. Our lives will have changed.

The roses in back are blooming now, remember them?
I wish I could send you one. I wish I could take them with me.

The kids and I sang rounds all weekend. Sarah mixes up the words
on purpose until we laugh so hard we can't go on.

You know how Geoff likes to talk about The Universe,
especially at bedtime?
                    He used to believe parents had the right
to kill their children. And he can't imagine growing up, he says,
therefore he must be doomed to die young.

Did it help to say I thought so too, once, and see how old I am?

He fell asleep, dirt streaking his wrists, creasing his throat
like one of the roses.
                    All this joy, my children growing up,
growing away. And loneliness, my old adversary.

You'll have to sleep with me come September. Your other choice
is the basement, a veritable pit of rats, snakes, or worse.
Summer's coming on. Lord. Let it be humorous.

Having Murdered 23 Slugs

As they surge from their froth-dreams
underground, under a rock, under a leaf,

whether born or hatched or fully formed
out of the deep grooves of their progenitors,

they raise their unbearably soft parts to feel whatever it is
they feel—not joy, surely, nor any of the abstract

thoughts we humans strain toward, but something more like
cold or damp, some sense of lett-us

as they slide toward what calls them finally.

Their lives are a continual falling. The spin-ache
we call gravity, they obey without
analysis, without the curious child's grave digging.

Where is death? Why do we need to practice it
here among the living? And yet
I am comforted.

Child of Slime, tongue of pure sensation,
I wash and wash my hands. A trace of you remains,
ineradicable, etched on the mind.

Fire in the Canyon

Past abandoned fire hoses coiled like rattlesnakes,
past the odor of death in its dank cave, past bodies of cacti
deflated upon themselves like Nefertiti's face: the curved, delicate

cartilage of a nose, mummified, horrible fin on a dark crust—
in the desert air, merciless, these visages rose
and mocked our beauty and our love.

Here had been paradise overgrown with vines,
desert grape clambering among the sycamore, cottonwood
leaves on their slender petioles scissoring the light.

Here the fan palms were ancient and thick. Their skirts
were homes for birds and animals.
The sound of them in the wind was like cool water.

Though it is months since the fire burned out of control,
we imagine we can feel the heat drumming in the ashes still.
A single yucca dares to bloom
and the tiny cactus fingers thrust out of the mounds.

The palms survive, stripped of their branches. A few green fans
have sprung out of the tops of them.
The owls have returned. The finches chatter as before.
And the river's running pure.

We strip and swim in its icy pools, gasping and shivering,
arching ourselves over the rocks to dry,
pale as two lizards underneath a wide, white sky.

The breeze carries a seed tuft
from place to place, soars past your loveliness,
your delta with its springs and pinks.

No Condors in Sight

We launch our bodies over the cliffs, our answering wings circle us up
three thousand feet to glide along the ancient flyways.

Over the spreading citrus, dry riverbeds of the Santa Clara and the Sespe,
over the small pink house,
a dog barks, a woman looks up.

Out of the sun's disk, black spots, black motionless wings sail west
forty miles, or northwest to the islands.

The dog barks, the woman raves, her children stretch into their lives.

We veer into a spiral laden with dark birds whose cries swell the air
as we descend to plunge into the rot-soft carcass
again and again

until the heart bursts and the maw lies open. Bloat and release, gorge
and surcease: there is enough.

Soaring the full, unruly winds of the Pacific, over the fields of bean
and sugar beet, startled towns, the pink house

where the father withers, over the laps of foothills, fossil shells
pushing out of the clay,
the new range

sheer by the old, wings whistling, fifty miles an hour we fly.

How Lightning Strikes

When hail beats down the ripening wheat,
as it sometimes does,
where can we turn our despair
except on those we love?
When we've kicked the cats and split hairs
and spat at our aging faces in the mirror,
what have we done?

The weather isn't fair.

It's also true that we don't deserve summer.
Here summer comes, ready or not,
and though we may hate loving it—
this pup the size of a grizzly bear
that romps on us and licks our necks,
there's no escape,

nothing to pay for the pleasure.

We stand here looking out to snowy peaks
in air so clear our eyes ache,
considering how a hunk of chalk scrapes against the slate,
and how the days remark, how nothing
stays the same, there's nothing we can keep,
and how lightning strikes

and isn't a punishment.

After the Crash,
the Old Fool Does Laundry

We've only to live it through, gracefully, I trust,
accepting these wintry mishaps for what they are.
The blouse blown against the fence is not a curse on us,
although it irritates us just as though it were.
And if you find me odd, and old, and even, therefore,
faintly disgusting, I find you callow, difficult to bear.
We are less indestructible than we at first appeared.
I belong to my desk and my disheveled floors,
to this droll celibacy, to the task of living alone here,
though not utterly chosen, nor altogether enforced,
more than I belong to you, who have come to my voice
as lover and nightmare, and who will be taken away,
not thank God by car crash, but daily as I make
my bed, sheets rinsed of event, and of memory.

A Real Mouse

This is how winter comes into our mile,
sleepily, sneakily over the buildings pours, while

workmen run with their shoulders hunched
in flimsy jackets and half-laced boots, somehow surprised,
pleased to be blown and in the world's waters drenched.

Full soft is the bed where I have slept, roused by living light
and light's alternate, with the approach of huge good luck, with God,

or what I know of God revealing itself over and over in flight.
For once, I'm satisfied: bills to write, verses in their folders tossed.

And still, beneath duty, beyond art, a real mouse darts
and cowers under the sink, hungers, gnaws teeth sharp.

Shorakkopoch

How deep is the mud? How big is the bay?
Why do you care to know?
It goes as far as it goes. It's difficult to say.

The heron came and fed, and went away
Elegantly fit to its shadow.
How deep is the mud? How big is the bay?

Rusts the upturned wheel, the abandoned cradle,
Sleeps the eel darkly by the plow.
It goes as far as it goes. It's difficult to say.

No gods in the hills, no inchoate, frail
Justice. A lonely flight of arrows.
How deep is the mud? How big is the bay?

We do not know how to be, but we pray
And wait. What else? And though
We go as far as we can go, it's difficult to say

Whether we ought to persist in these failed
Trysts. Who can help us? How
Deep is the mud? How big is the bay?
It goes as far as it goes. It's difficult to say.

The Way Corn Grows

In the courtyard, a leafless oak strung with colored lights.
Such a wee protest, a cry against the dark
that engulfs us as the whole earth tilts.

I have a pile of soft hats, gloves, scarves,
and a rack of coats arranged in order of warmth. I have my hours
marshaled and portioned into tasks,

cupboards where the moths thrive and where the mice
shop among jars of cinnamon and rice.

I have my trusted, companionable ghosts
with books under their arms, and with lamps to follow.

When the way is precarious,
when neither self-praise nor self-loathing tell me the truth,
I have only the world itself to lie down in.

The way corn grows, like giving birth.
The way vast migrations of geese sweep clean the eye that sees them.

Like Candles

Thinking on this rainy day of old lovers
like candles blown out on a cake.

I hate how life shrinks the huge fish I caught
and photographed, which ten years later
looks like a small perch, and the house I lived in once,
with its vaulted rooms, which turns out to be quite ordinary.

Even the ranch, which was my universe,
caught by a backward glance from the new highway
at seventy miles per hour as I speed toward my death,
is just a dimple in the hills, tilted and spinning away into space.

And the breasts, the areolas I woke to touch, the fragrances,
the silks and secrets, the bell voice breaking over me
like morning light: the fried egg happy on its plate
surfaces for a moment and slips away.

I don't know why, now my life is steady as a train on its track,
I regret what I lost. Like a coin tossed into a river of cash,

a dime I held and warmed in my fist,
I traded that for this.

Goodbye

Goodbye, dear Monster. I wish you well.
I hope you won't be judged by your scars.
With your eyes of all sizes and colors
you could be a lighthouse, or a prophet,
and though you have too many thumbs, and arms
that are short for your great bulk, you can love.

Am I not your mother?
And have't I scoured the planet all my life for such a heart?

I'll never forget how I found it in the rail yard
chuffing in its impatience to labor.
It was easy to find the redwoods, difficult
to drag them home and join them to your torso.

Over the years, how many children have I set
lumbering toward the village? And of those who returned,
how many odd parts are left
nodding, tapping toward some impossible future?

You are the last, and the best.
You may be wondering why I gave you breasts.
They are my own. Trust me.

Night Windows

The neighbors are making love again, their sighed, resonant cries
drawn out unexpectedly, honestly, into a summer night
that was longing for them, waiting to be filled.

My cats stir and shift on their pillows. And if,

at an exhibition, I am struck dumb standing in front of
Hopper's *Night Windows*, it is not by the half-dressed woman,
or the breeze that flies out of the painting and lifts my hair,

but by the love that renders them and strips them bare.

My own loves and failures, of which even now it is difficult to speak,
have been forgiven here. I can go on. I am not unlike
the happy man next door. I can hear him whistling in the shower.

In Phoebus' Car

> Here Phaeton lies: in Phoebus' car he fared,
> And though he greatly failed, more greatly dared.
>
> —Ovid

Remember that guy who strapped himself into a lawn chair
armed with a BB gun and a six-pack of Budweiser
and launched himself into the sky with twenty-eight weather
balloons like a small herd of lollipops wildly charging?
When the oxygen thinned, and ice began to form on him
and he had become a puzzling blip on the radar screen
at L.A. airport, diverting several large jet planes,
he shot eight balloons and sank through the smog, and tangled in
a power line. The fire department hauled him down and the
police department arrested him and the reporters
pushed toward him with their microphones to hear what he would say.

When the astronauts stepped out on the surface of the moon,
I was roaring down a bridge with my unhappy husband,
through the empty streets, wanting to see the moment, headlong
to his mother's house, where, in closets piled with old clothing,
we once hid, and stripped, and arched longingly toward our children.
I screamed for silence, I thought my husband was going to hit
me, I wanted to hear the first words spoken on the moon.

But I'm weary of disappointment. Let's talk about need:
starlings gathering in the trees outside, gripping the wires,
short-circuiting the TV screens, iridescent as oil,
greens darkly flashing purple, bristling bills and harsh, strong cries

Marriage

1

I wake up and put my head in the space between your breasts:
nowhere so safe, soft, nothing so fine, and warm skin underneath the shirt
you have on. You let me stay, god bless me, breathing dark and long
as the morning minutes turn, and then as I stretch free, you burrow in

with your face and hands, finding me, running your fingers around
and around. I curl for you, my girl, my lips above and below start to swell,
and then we tell our dreams and argue a while: who hogged the sheets,
who snored, who slept least, the purl and knit of our sweet-tart,
part-whole, sickness and health waking up together.

Time to go to work. The hot-pink panties I gave you as a joke
yank up your thighs and rump as you complain and pout.
Ah, how I mistreat you, my prize, my little sauerkraut.

Something is pulling you up out of our Saturday morning into the world
of your mind, that brute machine with its hard lips and thighs,
    eyes that see,
but not me, not my flesh, my bones, not the fact that I'm dying.

You're not curious but tolerant as you rise and grind and bring me a cup
to wake me. You're far out in the day, the next year, already running hard.
Your numbers flip like pennies' worth of gasoline. I want you to go,

I want you to zoom over your bright horizon, Jellybean, but give me
full five fathoms first, my fist, my submarine, give me a smack, a shine.

3

The great barge of you beached on my side of the bed, Lover, dammit,
it's my turn to sleep in. I like your company but sometimes I swear.
Like today when the first words I hear are angry words,
something you dreamed about your mother only she was me and anyway,
there there, I'm sure you had a perfect right to wake up bothered.

All I want is a little space. The world's going to hell and I'm getting older.
You're lying there solid as the hills and I'm trying to turn in my narrow row.
Sweetheart, I want you here. But sometimes I want you smaller,

quieter, nicer. I want you in my pocket, Dear.
I suppose I'm being unreasonable. It happens, but it's rare.

4

Mazatlán, Mexico

All those years of hiding what you feel, Protestant years
learning to keep control, and now I want you to peel and weep
and surge and crawl and beg for more, not proud, not tall and ironed
and showered and shined, but small and helpless once in a while.

I want you generous and shrill, fishwife and all, those wide thighs
high as the hills, the very grass groaning as it grows,
breaking in its needy silky sigh. I'm so far away. Write me,

but make the paper wet, I want sweat and shit and fingernails and hair,
wildflowers and slime folded up together, wildlife, not tame toast and tea.
Lover, I'm alone here in paradise, alone and queer and greedy.

5

I want you to take me back, now that I'm back, now that I'm here,
and you do. You've forgiven me for the little things that wear and tear.
You've taken me in like a bad brother. You've inhaled me like a temper,

slept with me while my knots and whorls worked loose and I mourned
the empty spaces, washed me with water and oil
like the feet of Christ or a wood floor. How can I fail?

I always thought that if I fell, I would be ridiculed, or left in my puddle.
But when I goof up, you love me more because I need it more.
If I had the art to say this new, I'd start a religion, or a war.

Sometimes it's tedious. I'm pissed because you push me away,
not flirtatious, not crisp but limp lettuce, lukewarm tea. *Is it age?*
I wonder, *Is it me?* Or is this the fate of the too-long together?

We become like sisters, like mother-daughter, old maid friends
squabbling equitably over breakfast, coughing up phlegm,
and then when I see you naked: nothing. Less than nothing.

A chill reminds me we're growing more frail, that the end,
though not soon, is just over the hill. Not the end of us together,
but of fascination, of rolling wild on the floor. Did we ever?

Or was it just a dream I thought we shared: two mild-mannered
ordinary women turning to sweet beasts in bed.
What was your dream? Two women knitting, cooking?
Christ, you make me so mad.

Or else it comes down to companionship, and the way we touch,
not urgent so much as sensuous, the way we scratch each other's backs
and say it's better than sex, almost, has to be enough. And it is,
somehow, though it might not be if it were all there was.

So much I want to say about love, the way I bank the coals
in the wood stove, or the way I rake up piles of leaves and leave them
to smolder, almost smother the small fire underneath, and allow the burn
to slowly fill the yard, the whole day, the whole life if I'm lucky.

We touch for comfort and pleasure, and yes it's still there—
not the need to snatch and tear but the underground warm waters
of eternal measure, the source in which we bathe
and of which we drink at our leisure.

Warm blood and warm water rushing through the rivers of your body
to your fingertips, to your toes, coursing down your sweeps of thighs
and calves, wide as your wrists, your spread hands and on into the day.

You warm the sheets, the room, my side of the bed, you warm the water
in the tub where I bathe after you like a pup, like a dog adoring.
And like a dog I eat you up, my food, my god, my green pastures,
the way you throw back your head, pretend you're tied
    and let me have you,
pried, unslung, disjointed and hung out in the sun, my vegetarian.

Spring springs from you, you tricky fool, pointing to the daffodils
as if you didn't know perfectly well what you'd done,
with your arms sprawled and your breasts hung low and your drawl.

IV

I was driven because I wanted to be like others.
I was afraid of what was wild and indecent in me.

—Czeslaw Milosz, *The Separate Notebooks*

Devil, Dear

The eternal bus goes by and in its dust,
roosters, dogs, children in their blue
and white uniforms walking home from school.

The madness has passed
and I wake in my own body, in Mexico.

Every other life seems small to me now,
shells I've struggled out of, parched along the trail
to this last place. Here, here I'll rest awhile.

Here I'll make a garden that I'll watch grow.
Here the bats circle at night. Lizards live on the wall.
And they sing, they really sing!

Four toucans have come also.
My neighbor points one out to me there, posed
by the window glass, with itself companionable.

We are proud they have come, proud that our barrio
was touched by these bright beaks and wings.

In spite of our murderous hearts, our greed, our neglect,
when we see him there, so simply stark,
we want to be careful, we want to keep his secret.

One day I hear his soft call
like drumsticks rasping on chocolate.

Three little girls on the shared wall
of my garden talk to the pretty cat.

They introduce themselves, for they are polite:
Rosaria, Estefania, Ariadnia, nieces of my neighbor the Greek,
and tiptoe on my red roof and sweep the leaves
away for me, careful not to fall.
But if they fell I'd catch them: leaves, light, and ringlets.

Above us on the barren peak, the Devil of this place,
one leg like a chicken, one leg like a goat,
does not sing his songs of praise.

They drove him away, the poor guy,
they planted a cross, they sprinkled holy water.

But we had what we had, didn't we, Devil, Dear?
With our mismatched limbs we danced, with our hoarse throats
we sang, we flew, we rode, we misbehaved.

Oh little girls, little girls, take heart!
Be brave!

Roosters

One sounds like he's just beginning to crow after an adolescence
dancing or harrying the hens or thinking perhaps he *was* a hen.
What was the difference between them? Just a hairsbreadth comb
placed fleshily on the crack of his cranium, odd as a single labium,
alert, sunburned, now unaccountably growing. Is this the flag of rooster
hood, or is it these tail feathers black and green as certain inks?

In these past two days, he feels the need for voice, for practice
though he has nothing important to announce. Oh, the sunrise, yes,
but also the damp dirt asquirm with insect life, the hose left
snaking out uncoiled all night. He heralds twilight, sounds mammalian—
not quite car-hit dog, not child being maimed, not cat rent by feline
passion, but some new sound breaking out of its membrane.

Carmen and her cousin have not spoken for three years over a trivial
misunderstanding that might have been avoided had either been
willing to change her position. Then Carmen split with her girlfriend.
Then her mother's leg was cut off due to diabetes and gangrene.
They too had been estranged, but Carmen rushed to her mother's bed.
Her mother said she'd have given both legs to get Carmen back again.

The photos of myself taken just a day ago for the immigration forms
already seem alien, as blood seems once it is drawn from the vein
and bagged in plastic and labeled with black pen. Though it is still
warm from my body, it soon chills, mixed with a salt, laid uncere-
moniously on a shelf. I'm lonely for that self, stilled and fraught with
secret meanings, where I sat on a stool, exposed and faintly ridiculous.

Yet the woman didn't care who I was as she slapped the cold roll of
film into her camera. She wanted my shoulders straight, my chin up,
my eyes not to close. But when I look at the blotchy skin of my cheeks,
my sunburned nose, I see my whole family—a grandmother I didn't
know, her profile like my profile, small chin, wattle of skin below,
the slumped shoulders and neck thrust unaggressively forward.

I want to be loved in that posture, to be found handsome even though
my heavy breasts pull me down and the hours I spend at my desk
make my shoulders slope. Like everyone else, I want to be adored.
I still carry such foolish, unquenchable hope. That tousled haircut
and green, cotton shirt are not me, though I did sit there for a moment.
She is contained, that woman with the lined neck, but I have flown out.

There's An Engine

There's an engine in the distance,
an engine I can't quite identify, whether hovering or warming,
climbing or descending, grinding or cooling or pushing water.

There's an engine rolling the beds, an engine under the city,
in the drains, in the waves.

There's an engine in the body making cells, whether for good
or for evil, whether for healing or for killing, there's an engine.

There's an engine in the dog, urgent in the rooster and in the tuning.
Fans hum, insects feed and lay their eggs on pails and mop strings.
Who can wait for rain?

Sometimes I love and sometimes I can't love what carries me.
Like a child, I praise what gives and revile what takes away.

I pray to the engine for mercy: on me, on those I need, mercy
for strangers, for nations, mercy for the spankers
and mercy for the killers of souls.

I pray to the watchmaker to set me slow, to slow down the tumblers
tumbling in the locks, the waters falling past pillows.

I pray for the body to last a little longer:
your body, my body, our body.

Moon, Scorpion, Fish Heads, Wind

The moon rises over the town, there in the east with her reflected shine: present, aware, patient, absorptive—an eye, the blank eye of a fish in the inky ocean. She watches. She never says a word. Through all of time, never a word from the moon.

We know so little about how things happen. Fish heads appear on my roof again, and in the garden. Scorpions appear on the roof, and always after one of the high, sudden winds. It's the time of wind-borne plagues. We suffer from parasites—amoebas, and let me say it: worms. We take vile medicines. We cough and sweat our change-borne fevers. This is the time of heat, the dry spring that bears us toward the oncoming summer rains.

After the first rain, the old time farmers plant corn, *milpas*: corn plus squash plus beans. They poke with a stick, drop the seed, and tread on it to set it in the ground. Women and children sell the blue corn *gorditas, little fat ones*, that I heat on the griddle and split and stuff with whatever I have around. This morning it was scrambled eggs, but sometimes it's beans and onions and tomatoes and cilantro, or sautéed young nopal paddles, usually sold by the same little girls who swindle me twice a week or so. Ten pesos is twice the going rate, but I have the money, and they need it more than I.

Today, again, the cats crunch on fish heads. Lola, my helper, says the neighbors throw them over onto my roof. But the fish heads are odorless, like parchment, dry and crisp as air can make them. And they always appear this time of year, after a high wind. Lola says the scorpions come on the wind, so why not fish heads? They are the same chitinous substance, light as leaves. I think of them flickering in the wind, spinning until, click, they hit against the highest object on the hill, which is my house, which is the set-back wall over the stairway to the roof, a perfect catch-place. I mean to ask my neighbors if they find them too, but when I remember to ask, the neighbors aren't home, and when they're home, I don't remember.

The scorpions land here, very much alive, and grand in size. They are the brown ones, and when I was stung last year, it was less than the sting of a bee. But there are others: blonde ones, black ones, and some are lethal, apparently. It's hard to know what to believe. Everyone has an opinion, and none of them agree. Or sometimes they agree. I shake out my shoes. I shake the towel before drying myself, as that's how I was stung.

My life is passing strange. I look at the moon. It seems as though I'm inside the womb seeing the ovum shining there. Am I the soul of myself watching my own conception?

When I was stung by the scorpion, I had been mad all day. The last time I felt that angry a cancer appeared, a melanoma on the back of my arm. I knew that such anger was dangerous to me, and that I must make a change. I stepped out of the bath and grabbed a towel and began to dry my back, and felt a series of small stings on my wrist, as if with a sharp hair. I dropped the towel as my forearm began to throb, and the small brown scorpion, dazed and dazzled by my rubbing it against myself, fell to the floor. I ran for a shoe and crushed it. It died easily, didn't run away.

My arm began to swell. Just then a friend arrived, the woman with whom I was so angry. She seemed amused, or revenged, by the fact that I had been stung. It was as if, in her mind, I was stung by my own anger.

I wondered if she was right, because the inner world and the outer world often mirror each other. Perhaps they always do. We have so many proofs that other people have thought in the same way: the *I Ching*, the many forms of augury, entrails, astrology. Leaves settle into the bottom of a cup of tea, and some people see images there. I may have seen them too.

My wrist stopped hurting. I wasn't choking on my tongue or feeling ill, so I went on with my day. But the sting killed some of my flesh, which itched unbearably, until, months later, I had scratched it all away.

Across the street, Clara, our local soprano who grew up in Maine, is singing one of the arias from *Madama Butterfly*. The Japanese woman singing in Italian. My life is passing strange.

This cobblestoned street, these scorpions and fish heads, the moon now directly overhead and full, the glue-sniffing teenagers and children shouting as they kick a tattered soccer ball, the young tender greens soaking in a bowl. They've taken in sunlight and transpired water all day into the atmosphere. What to make of it all? What's happening here?

Disco Saturday Night

1.

One night in August, after a full two months of tropical heat,
almost unnoticed in the glamour and glare, after a lifetime
of swimming more or less alone, she glides in to the beach and strikes
sand and drags herself straight out of the water thirty yards
    and starts to dig.

A crowd gathers, women with their shoes held in their hands,
men in white shirts and leather. Someone has called the Harbor Police.
Stand back, stand back, give her air, give her room.

By now she has made a shallow basin and has turned and started to lay.
She has barely arrived in time.

Wet and ripe, the white orbs pile over one another, each one deliberate,
each one important as the crowd murmurs and the cars slow down
and her eyes, glazed, seem not to see, not to understand,
her urge so strong, so compelling.

She defecates and begins pushing sand over the nest with her paddles,
pushing, pushing, and then begins her trip back to the waves,
half-lifted and hurried along by the Harbor Police
who will dig up her eggs to incubate them.

When she hits the first wave, she lifts a little, then keeps crawling
and hits the second wave, suddenly lithe and free,
and with a few strong thrusts, escapes the light, the noise, the task,
the scent of dogs and rats, and disappears headlong into the sea.

2.

It was not the thing itself.
It should not have been remarkable.

A hundred years in the past nobody would have noticed
or stopped to watch one female among thousands, one nest
with its Ping-Pong balls faintly luminous.

We would have been digging, shoveling the piles of unborn islands,
continents into a bag to be eaten without guilt,
seasoned with lime juice and salt, lips smacked and singing.

It was inexhaustible. It was a universe.
It was like a woman giving herself for the first time every time,
like sex that comes and goes and comes again, it was a divine food.

How could anyone have turned away from what was offered
and what was so clearly good?

3.

The turtle swims alone out of the wide bay — overhead the swells,
greens and yellows filtered by clouds of kelp, shadows of grey whales,
whole herds moving with one mind to the warm waters

where they will give birth, females spurting single child-whales,
shimmying free in shoals of blood, turning and nuzzling
    them up to the air,
hosed clouds of milk in the water nurturing the small ones
as they bump and swim together, lumbering into the shallows,
    resting there.

The turtle swims on, feeds and dives with her broad paddles pulling her.
She does not think about her sons and daughters curled
    in their paper shells,
the life throbbing in the jellied forms, the idea of turtle constant in them,
the need to be cooled by the tide and warmed by the sun.

She does not ask for anything, but leaves them there, impassive, trusting.
Hours ago she had already forgotten.

Letter from Paradise

I want you to know that I found happiness
alive in little boys in Mazatlán at the summer solstice
when the tides had tipped from one end of the beach
and left the sand in a crescent cliff exactly like the moon,

Mother, a crescent cliff exactly like the moon.

I saw a dozen little boys, not a girl-child among them, orphans perhaps,
or shoeshine experts, or gum salesmen, or acrobats
who should have been in school.

The waves crashed them into the sand, and counter-waves
peaked and slopped and sloshed them, washed them.

And then a crushing tree trunk heaved toward where they swam.

Twelve little boys, each with an arm and leg to be maimed,
each with a chest full of air, with me wanting to warn them away,

rode and plunged and climbed and fell and slipped and escaped
and hung on.

Life's tragic face—the arrows shot straight up
fell somewhere else, somewhere the boys didn't care about.

They were there on the beach, carried in and out
while the sun sank and the day got dark, not stopping to rest,
pulling their pants up and running right back forever.

Baja Eclogue

1.

This was what we saw: the far waters' reach to mountains so bleak
they were mythic, slabs of blue and maroon changing hue
as the light changed, as if they were part of our minds,
as if our minds were elemental.

A huge weight was shifting in us, grief, lust, loss,
upwelling oil, burning minerals and salts.

We touched and slept, we moved our two plates from table to sink,
we were born, we gave birth, we plunged and leapt,
around us were the cries of birds and whales gasping as they surfaced.

2.

After a while we could recognize a whale under the boat
or in the near distance by the pale mass sometimes moving sometimes still,
but we couldn't tell how deep it was or what it might do next.

There was an immanence, a barely perceptible bulge or heave
in the imagination or in the sea—it was hard to tell which was which
from our small craft—and after a while our longing was such
that it didn't matter anyway.

With us were two young people, a couple more fixed
on each other than on anything else.

They had discovered sex, invented it actually, and were so caught
in their mutual fascination that the rest of the world was dull,
even this most remarkable hour they might ever pass.

You and I have lived long enough to know
that the erotic has a life apart from its participants,

that it can move away from us and return just as surprisingly,
and that we are no more in control of its comings and goings
than we are of the weather. We know, or think we know what to do,
the way a nun lights candles, dresses ritually in the cold

and makes her way to the sanctuary. She falls on her knees
and begins the loved movements of mind, tongue, throat, hands.

Yet grace, when it comes, is still a mystery.
We can seek, but we cannot find.

3.

Where did we think we were going? Southward, toward the Cape,
then across to Mazatlán. To say, unequivocally,
we were moving across a landscape, is not to say anything.

We spent our days with fingers on maps, tracing skin, we bathed
and ate, we swam over the surface while shy stingrays
lifted from the sand and fluttered away. The floor of the bay
was populated with little clams called *chocolates*.

So this is how it happens: words fall away.
What we don't know, Beloved, we don't learn.
This is what it means to dream that we are in the world.

4.

Then we crossed at night over the deep mouth of the Sea of Cortez,
first me, then you, pressing your face into the salt atmosphere.

Under the moon, in the bruised boat, I saw you look up in surprise
and delight, and only the thin walls of the room kept me from flying out.

Not what we did there in the narrow bunk,
but how the swells tipped us toward one another, how we drank
and nothing was spilled, and nothing left over.

Crickets

They were travelers, but they always came back
on a warm summer night, drenched in mathematics,
singing like a unison of stars on the lake.

There's a hut at the end of a field where I and the dogs
sometimes walk. Two shirts on a line. No electric light.
It is shaded by the widest, tallest tree, older than our street.

I miss my father late at night and think of my old companions,
how everything they taught was true and bright
and of how we are still on earth together, still wide awake.

Notes

"Shorakkopoch"

Shorakkopoch Rock marks the tidal basin in the Inwood area of New York City where, supposedly, Manhattan Island was bought from the Lenape tribe for a shipment of goods worth sixty guilders. I think several other locations in Manhattan also make similar claims.

"The Children of John Farlo's Wife"

John Farlo and his Native wife, whose name was not known, were occasionally seen in the mountains of Baja, California. They rode into our camp once when we were in the Sierra Madre. The wife was very tall, unwashed, beautiful, and fierce. The men (my uncles and grandfather and Epifanio, the ranch foreman) became quite nervous in her presence, as she was reputed to be very good with a knife. One of her descendants claims to be related to us by way of a connection between her and my great-grandfather, possibly at knife-point. We like the story a lot. However, it has nothing to do with the poem, which is based on a different story about her that the men told after she and John Farlo had ridden away.

"Moon, Scorpions, Fish Heads, Wind"

The lines "my life is passing strange" were originally spoken by Shakespeare's Ophelia.

"Faith in Nights"

This poem is titled after Joel Harrison's musical composition.

Recent Titles from Alice James Books

Eros Is More, Juan Antonio González Iglesias, Translated by Curtis Bauer

Mad Honey Symposium, Sally Wen Mao

Split, Cathy Linh Che

Money Money Money | Water Water Water, Jane Mead

Orphan, Jan Heller Levi

Hum, Jamaal May

Viral, Suzanne Parker

We Come Elemental, Tamiko Beyer

Obscenely Yours, Angelo Nikolopoulos

Mezzanines, Matthew Olzmann

Lit from Inside: 40 Years of Poetry from Alice James Books,
Edited by Anne Marie Macari and Carey Salerno

Black Crow Dress, Roxane Beth Johnson

Dark Elderberry Branch: Poems of Marina Tsvetaeva,
A Reading by Ilya Kaminsky and Jean Valentine

Tantivy, Donald Revell

Murder Ballad, Jane Springer

Sudden Dog, Matthew Pennock

Western Practice, Stephen Motika

me and Nina, Monica A. Hand

Hagar Before the Occupation | Hagar After the Occupation,
Amal al-Jubouri

Pier, Janine Oshiro

Heart First into the Forest, Stacy Gnall

This Strange Land, Shara McCallum

lie down too, Lesle Lewis

Panic, Laura McCullough

Milk Dress, Nicole Cooley

Parable of Hide and Seek, Chad Sweeney

Shahid Reads His Own Palm, Reginald Dwayne Betts

How to Catch a Falling Knife, Daniel Johnson

Phantom Noise, Brian Turner

Father Dirt, Mihaela Moscaliuc

Pageant, Joanna Fuhrman

The Bitter Withy, Donald Revell

Winter Tenor, Kevin Goodan

Alice James Books has been publishing poetry since 1973. The press was founded in Boston, Massachusetts as a cooperative wherein authors performed the day-to-day undertakings of the press. This collaborative element remains viable even today, as authors who publish with the press are also invited to become members of the editorial board and participate in editorial decisions at the press. The editorial board selects manuscripts for publication via the press's annual, national competition, the Alice James Award. Alice James Books seeks to support women writers and was named for Alice James, sister to William and Henry, whose extraordinary gift for writing went unrecognized during her lifetime.

Designed by Pamela A. Consolazio
LITTLE FROG DESIGNS

Printed by Book Mobile